Robyn Hood of Deadwood

a cowboy (and cowgirl)
musical for kids

by Richard Free

with additional material
by Peter Shrubshall

A SAMUEL FRENCH ACTING EDITION

SAMUEL FRENCH

FOUNDED 1830

SAMUELFRENCH.COM
SAMUELFRENCH-LONDON.CO.UK

FOR PRODUCTION ENQUIRIES

UNITED STATES AND CANADA
Info@SamuelFrench.com
1-866-598-8449

UK, EUROPE AND THE REST OF THE WORLD
Plays@SamuelFrench-London.co.uk
020-7255-4302/01

Each title is subject to availability from Samuel French, depending upon country of performance. Please be aware that ROBYN HOOD OF DEADWOOD may not be licensed by Samuel French in your territory. Producers should contact the nearest Samuel French office or licensing partner to verify availability.

ROBYN HOOD OF DEADWOOD was first workshopped at Belmont Junior School, Tottenham, London.

It was premiered in 2013 by Organised Kaos, a theatre group for 7-11 year olds, under the leadership of Alison Wood and Suzy Davies.

If you enjoy this show, take a look at *Around The Pond In 80 Days*, by Shrubshall & Free, also published by Samuel French.

CHARACTERS

ROBYN HOOD – the notorious female outlaw
MARION WAYNE – a wanderin' cow<u>boy</u>

THE MERRY GALS

LILLIAN 'LILL' JOHN – Robyn's right-hand gal
FREYA 'THE FRYER' TUCK – the cook
WILHEMINA 'WILL' SCARLET – bloodthirsty outlaw
ELEANOR DALE – the balladeer
MINDY 'MUCH' MILLERSON – sweet but not too bright
MARY
MOIRA
MERCY
MARCY
MURIEL
EUPHEMIA

THE BADDIES

JOHN PRINCE – cattle baron
SHERIFF NOTTINGHAM – dumb lawman
GUY GISBOURNE – Deputy, even dumberer than the Sheriff
DEPUTIES 1, 2, 3, 4, 5 & 6

THE INDIANS (girls or boys)

CHIEF MOUNTAIN LION HEART
RUNNING BEAR
HOWLING WOLF
SQUATTING DOG

WESTERN FOLK

DOC – the doctor
SHARPSHOOTER X – illiterate shooter
SHARPSHOOTER DAN – Swedish shooter
BALLADEER BETTY
BALLADEER BELLE
TOWNSFOLK 1, 2, 3, 4, 5 & 6
Assorted Townsfolk & Indians

SONG LIST

Backing tracks and orchestral parts are available on hire from Samuel French. Please enquire.

THE SHOW

This is a show for kids around 10-14 years of age. The songs are mostly chorus numbers where lines can be sung solo if there is the vocal talent. Although it is about cowboys (and cowgirls) no one shoots a gun, only catapults – however, the pillow fight at the end can get quite rowdy.

The action takes place in the Wild West town of Deadwood – ruled by John Prince, a cattle baron, and Sheriff Nottingham – and also the surrounding area of Loxley County, home to those notorious outlaws, Robyn Hood and the Merry Gals.

Sets can be realised or suggested with lighting changes and simple props. However, there should be a stack of pillows 'dressed' as sacks of oats laid at the back of the stage.

Working with Organised Kaos theatre group, we cast a girl to play John Prince. Disliking asking girls to play boys or boys to play girls, I changed John to Joan and 'he' to 'she', but I also had to change some lyrics in *Vote For Me*. I have provided alternative lyrics in case the same situation arises.

Richard Free
www.freemusicals.co.uk

For my wife

Scene I

(Cast enter and sing in three chorus canon, **THE BALLAD OF ROBYN HOOD***)*

(CHORUS 1)   *(CHORUS 2)*   *(CHORUS 3)*

(CHORUS 1)	*(CHORUS 2)*	*(CHORUS 3)*
ROBYN, ROBYN,	ROBYN, ROBYN,	ROBYN, ROBYN,
ROBYN, ROBYN,	ROBYN,	ROBYN, ROBYN,
ROBYN,	ROBYN,	ROBYN, ROBYN,
ROBYN,	ROBYN,	ROBYN, ROBYN,
ROBYN,	ROBYN,	ROBYN...
ROBYN,	ROBYN...	
ROBYN...		

CAST.

ROBYN,
ROBYN HOOD,
ROBYN HOOD OF DEADWOOD,
ROBYN,
ROBYN HOOD,
ROBYN HOOD OF DEADWOOD.

BORN TO A FARMER AND HIS PRETTY WIFE,
ROBYN PLANNED TO LIVE A CAREFREE LIFE,
'TIL MASKED MEN CAME AND STOLE THE FARM AWAY,
ROBYN SWORE THERE'D BE REVENGE SOMEDAY.

AND THE NAME IS ROBYN,
ROBYN HOOD,
ROBYN HOOD OF DEADWOOD,
ROBYN,
ROBYN HOOD,
ROBYN HOOD OF DEADWOOD.

BOTH PARENTS DRIVEN TO AN EARLY GRAVE,
BRANDED AS AN OUTLAW BY THE NOT-SO-BRAVE,
ROBYN RESIGNED TO SETTLE EV'RY SCORE

BY STEALING FROM THE RICH AND GIVING TO THE POOR,

(CHORUS 1 & 2)	*(CHORUS 3)*
AND THE NAME IS ROBYN,	ROBYN,
ROBYN HOOD,	ROBYN HOOD,
ROBYN HOOD OF DEADWOOD,	ROBYN HOOD OF DEADWOOD,
ROBYN,	ROBYN,
ROBYN HOOD,	ROBYN HOOD...
ROBYN HOOD OF DEADWOOD.	OF DEADWOOD.
ROBYN,	ROBYN,
ROBYN HOOD,	ROBYN HOOD,
ROBYN HOOD OF DEADWOOD,	ROBYN HOOD OF DEADWOOD,
ROBYN,	ROBYN,
ROBYN HOOD,	ROBYN HOOD...
ROBYN HOOD OF DEADWOOD,	OF DEADWOOD,
ROBYN HOOD OF DEADWOOD,	ROBYN HOOD OF DEADWOOD,
ROBYN HOOD OF DEADWOOD.	ROBYN HOOD OF DEADWOOD.

(cast exit)

Scene II

(Deadwood)

(**TOWNSFOLK** *go about their everyday business.*
SHERIFF, **GISBOURNE** *&* **DEPUTIES** *mill about.* **JOHN
PRINCE** *enters furtively.*)

JOHN PRINCE. Sheriff. Sheriff Nottingham.

SHERIFF. Mornin', John.

GISBOURNE. Mornin', Mister Prince.

DEPUTIES. Mornin'.

JOHN PRINCE. *(secretively)* Quiet down, will ya? I just rode in
to Deadwood because…

SHERIFF. You rode in? But where's your horse, John?

JOHN PRINCE. I left it tied up. Just over there.

(**JOHN PRINCE** *points off. FX: a horse neighs*)

GISBOURNE. That's a mighty fine looking beast, Mister
Prince.

JOHN PRINCE. Like I say, I <u>rode</u> in because I have some very
important and very secret news.

SHERIFF/DEPUTIES. *(quite loudly)* <u>News</u>?

GISBOURNE. Heck, real honest-to-goodness <u>news</u>?

SHERIFF. *(to* **GISBOURNE***)* That's what the man said, Guy.
Man like John Prince don't promise <u>news</u> when he
ain't got no <u>news</u> to speak of.

JOHN PRINCE. *(shushing them)* Will you keep it down? What
I've got to say can't be broadcast to the whole town.

(**SHERIFF** *&* **GISBOURNE** *lean in*)

JOHN PRINCE. You remember that stretch of river I…
(thinks)…inherited?

SHERIFF. You mean the river you took off old man Hood
when you stole his land?

DEPUTY 1 & 2. And his farmhouse.

DEPUTY 3 & 4. And his henhouse.

DEPUTY 5 & 6. And his outhouse.

GISBOURNE. Poor fella just had nowhere left to go.

JOHN PRINCE. *(coughs loudly to interrupt them)* Like I say, the stretch of river I <u>inherited</u>. Well, I happened to be fishing in it this morning and noticed something sparkling in the water. Don't say a word to anyone, but I started panning, and there in the bottom of my pan I found a whole stack of gold.

SHERIFF/GISBOURNE/DEPUTIES. *(loudly)* Gold?

JOHN PRINCE. I said not to say a word.

(The **TOWNSFOLK** *lift their heads as if they can smell something on the wind)*

JOHN PRINCE. *(cont.)* If these Deadwood deadbeats get a whiff of it, I'll have every panhandler and horn-swoggler tearing up the place to get their hands on my gold.

SHERIFF/GISBOURNE/DEPUTIES. Gold?!

JOHN PRINCE. I said to keep it down!

*(***TOWNSFOLK** *turn to each other. They know something's up but don't know what it is)*

JOHN PRINCE. There's so much of the stuff, I'm going to have to sneak it out of town in order not to raise suspicions. I'm going to need you and your deputies to smuggle small quantities of gold...

SHERIFF/GISBOURNE/DEPUTIES. Gold?!!

JOHN PRINCE. Will you please shut up?!

(It's too late. **TOWNSFOLK** *start to sing.* **GOLD FEVER IN OLD DEADWOOD***)*

TOWNSFOLK.
> GOLD, GOLD, GOLD, GOLD,
> GOLD, GOLD, GOLD, GOLD,
> GOLD, GOLD, GOLD, GOLD,
> GOLD, GOLD, GOLD, GOLD,
> WE WANT GOLD,
> JUST ONE NUGGET,
> THE SMALLEST GRAIN
> WE'LL KISS AND HUG IT,
> THAT YELLOW METAL'S WHAT WE WANT TO HOLD,
> GIVE US JUST A LITTLE,
> OR A LOT, OR A POT,
> OR A SACK, OR A STACK OF GOLD.

*(**DOC** enters, inspects people, looking in their ears and eyes and feeling their pulses)*

TOWNSFOLK.
> GOLD, GOLD, GOLD, GOLD,
> GOLD, GOLD, GOLD, GOLD,
> GOLD, GOLD, FEVER,
> FEVER,

DOC. My word. This is terrible. This is the worst case I've ever seen of Midas Malarial Miasma. Or, in layman's terms, <u>gold fever</u>!

TOWNSFOLK.
> THE DOCTOR'S FOUND A CASE OF
> GOLD FEVER IN OLD DEADWOOD,
> THE TEMP'RATURE IS UP HIGH,
> NO TREATMENT FOR GOLD FEVER,
> WITHOUT A CURE WE MAY DIE.

> WE NEED GOLD IN OUR POCKET,
> A GREAT BIG STASH, AWAY WE'LL LOCK IT,
> LIKE KING SOLOMON IN DAYS OF OLD,
> WE COULD HAVE A MINE, MAKE A MINT, FOLK'D SQUINT
> AT THE SHINE FROM OUR GLITTERING GOLD.

> WE'RE REALLY COMING DOWN WITH...
> GOLD FEVER IN OLD DEADWOOD,
> THE TEMP'RATURE IS UP HIGH,
> NO TREATMENT FOR GOLD FEVER,
> WITHOUT A CURE WE MAY DIE.

TOWNSFOLK.

WE LOVE GOLD!

SHERIFF/GISBOURNE/DEPUTIES.

WE NEED SOMETHING ALCHEMIC

TOWNSFOLK.

GOTTA HAVE GOLD!

SHERIFF/GISBOURNE/DEPUTIES.

IT'S REACHING EPIDEMIC!

TOWNSFOLK.

GOLD,
GOLD,
GOLD, GOLD,
GOLD, GOLD,
GOLD FEVER, GOLD FEVER,
GOLD! GOLD! GOLD! GOLD!

JOHN PRINCE. *(sneakily)* But we've got to watch out for that outlaw, Robyn Hood. If word gets round we're sneaking loot out of town, that bothersome bandit is bound to try and nab my gold.

JOHN PRINCE. Are you chuckleheads even listening to me?

CAST.

WE CAUGHT A NASTY DOSE OF…
GOLD FEVER IN OLD DEADWOOD,
THE TEMP'RATURE IS UP HIGH,
NO TREATMENT FOR GOLD FEVER,
WITHOUT A CURE WE MAY DIE.
GOLD FEVER IN OLD DEADWOOD,
THE TEMP'RATURE IS UP HIGH,
NO TREATMENT FOR GOLD FEVER,
WITHOUT A CURE,
WE'RE PRETTY SURE THAT
WITHOUT A CURE WE SURELY
DIE, DIE, DIE, DIE,
DIE, DIE, DIE, DIE,
DIE, DIE, DIE, DIE,
DIE!

JOHN PRINCE. *(to* **TOWNSFOLK***)* Oh, you folks think I said 'gold'. No, no, no. I was simply saying how I discovered…<u>mould</u>. Yep, that's what I said, <u>mould</u>. In the bottom of my <u>pans</u>. I found mould in my pans and now I've had to sack my dishwasher. That's all. So you can just go about your business. There's no gold. Never was. Just mould. Now, go on. Git goin'.

*(***TOWNSFOLK*** speak as they exit.)*

TOWNSFOLK 1. I could've sworn he said 'gold'.

TOWNSFOLK 2. Me too. Well I guess 'gold' is pretty close to 'mould'.

TOWNSFOLK 3. Shows how easy it is to get stuff wrong.

TOWNSFOLK 4. 'Specially when they sound so similar.

TOWNSFOLK 5. I feel a little silly having sung that song now.

TOWNSFOLK 6. Oh, I don't think anyone noticed.

(They exit.)

DOC. John Prince, it really is a blessing that you're such a devious devil…and that the townsfolk of Deadwood are such dazzling dunderheads.

JOHN PRINCE. Darn tootin', Doc.

(All exit.)

Scene III

(Echo Canyon. **MARION** *enters with the* **BALLADEERS**.*)*

MARION. *(to off)* Stay there, Shadow. You can't come with me through Echo Canyon.

(FX: a horse neighs)

MARION. *(cont.)* Good horse.

*(***MARION*** *and* ***BALLADEERS*** *sing.* **WANDERIN' COWBOY**)*

MARION/BALLADEERS.
I'M/HE'S JUST A WANDERIN' COWBOY,
ALWAYS RIDIN' THE TRAIL,

(FX: a horse neighs)

EXCEPT WHEN I'M/HE'S SADDLE-WEARY,
THEN MY/HIS BOOTS NEVER FAIL.
SEE I'M/HE'S A WANDERIN' COWBOY...

MERRY GALS. *(off, as echo)*
A WANDERIN' COWBOY...

MARION/BALLADEERS. *(looking around, surprised at the echo)*
FREE TO GO TOWN TO TOWN...

MERRY GALS. *(off)*
FREE TO GO TOWN TO TOWN...

MARION. So that's why they call this Echo Canyon.

MARION/BALLADEERS.
NO-ONE CAN TELL ME/HIM MY/HIS BUSINESS...

MERRY GALS. *(off)*
CAN'T TELL HIM NOTHIN'...

MARION/BALLADEERS.
NO-ONE WILL EVER PIN ME/HIM DOWN...

MERRY GALS. *(off)*
CAN'T PIN HIM DOWN.

LILL. *(off)* Pin him down, gals!

*(***MERRY GALS*** *enter and overpower* ***MARION***)*

MARION. Let go a' me! Let go a' me, you no-account sidewinders!

WILL. Now, that ain't a nice way to talk to a lady.

MARION. *(realising they are girls)* You mean…? Wait a minute! You're girls!

TUCK. You only just noticed?

MARION. Aw heck. I'm a rough, tough *hombre*, and I just been bushwhacked by a bunch a' women. Gee, I ain't fit to call myself a real cowboy.

ELEANOR. *(pointing to* **BALLADEERS***)* Why don't that bunch help you out?

BALLADEER BETTY. Oh, we're just his balladeers.

BALLADEERS BELLE. It's strictly a singing role.

WILL. So you're alone. I'd be mighty a'feared, if I was you.

MARION. I ain't the fearin' kind.

LILL. Maybe not, but you just hand over your loot and we promise not to say a word to the other cowboys 'bout you being robbed by girls.

MARION. *(fearful)* You wouldn't.

MARY. Oh, we would.

MARION. But I'm broke.

MOIRA. A likely story.

WILL. Let's beat it outta him.

    (**WILL** *&* **MERCY** *search his pockets)*

MARION. Honest. I don't have a red cent to my name.

MERCY. *(turning out his empty pockets)* He's right, Lill.

MUCH. Say, what is your name, cowboy? You look mighty familiar to me.

MARION. My name? My name's… *(thinks)*…Butch.

MARCY. You don't seem too sure about that…Butch.

MARION. Of course I'm sure. You think I don't know my own name? I'm Butch Wayne.

MUCH. Wayne? That's it. You're old Duke Wayne's boy. But I thought you was called Marion.

MERRY GALS. Marion?!

> (**MERRY GALS** *laugh.* **BALLADEERS** *look* **MARION** *up and down*)

MUCH. I don't see what's wrong with naming a fella Marion. I once knew a boy called Sue…*(thinks)*…or maybe it was Stew…

LILL. Well, <u>Marion</u>, we have a problem. If we return without any booty, our boss is gonna get awful mad.

MARION. Who's your boss? Can I speak to him and straighten this thing out?

MURIEL. You mean you don't know where you are?

EUPHEMIA. This here's Echo Canyon. In Loxley County.

TUCK. Home to that notorious outlaw…

MERRY GALS. Robyn Hood!

MARION. If you're trying to impress me, I can tell you I ain't the impressin' kind. 'Specially not by some two-bit hoodlum.

ELEANOR. Well, maybe this'll change your mind…

> (**MERRY GALS** *sing.* ***THE BALLAD OF ROBYN HOOD – REPRISE***)

MERRY GALS.

ROBYN,
ROBYN HOOD,
ROBYN HOOD OF DEADWOOD,
ROBYN,
ROBYN HOOD,
ROBYN HOOD OF DEADWOOD.

MANY'S THE STORIES OF ROBYN HOOD,
SOME ARE TRUE AND OTHERS ARE ALL WRONG,
FOLK HAVE GOT THE IDEA ROBYN AIN'T NO GOOD,
WE CAN PUT 'EM RIGHT IN THIS HERE SONG.

FOR MANY YEARS THE DAZZLING DESPERADO
'S BEEN HUNTED DOWN AND HOUNDED LIKE A CUR,
SO TRUTH HAS BEEN QUITE INCOMMUNICADO,
BUT YOU CAN'T BRAND AN IDEAL WITH A SLUR.

NOT ONE LIKE ROBYN,
ROBYN HOOD,
ROBYN HOOD OF DEADWOOD,
ROBYN,
ROBYN HOOD,
ROBYN HOOD OF DEADWOOD.

THIS SO-CALLED BANDIT WANTS TO SPREAD THE WEALTH
AROUND,
USES GAINS TO HELP THE POORER CLASS,
A NOBLE CAUSE TO FIGHT INJUSTICE WHEN IT'S FOUND,
'SPECIALLY IF THE LAW IS SUCH AN ASS.

MARION/BALLADEERS.

THIS ROBYN LEGEND SOUNDS A LOT A' HOOEY,
YOU GALS MUST THINK MY/HIS HEAD IS PRETTY THICK,
I'VE/HE'S GONE FROM *SAN ANTONE* TO OLD ST. LOUIS,
AND NEVER MET AN OUTLAW WORTH A LICK.

NO, NOT THIS ROBYN,
ROBYN HOOD,
ROBYN HOOD OF DEADWOOD,
ROBYN,
ROBYN HOOD,
ROBYN HOOD IS NO GOOD.

MERRY GALS.	**MARION/BALLADEERS.**
BUT THIS IS ROBYN,	ROBYN,
ROBYN HOOD,	ROBYN HOOD,
ROBYN HOOD OF DEADWOOD,	ROBYN HOOD IS NO GOOD,
ROBYN,	ROBYN,
ROBYN HOOD,	ROBYN HOOD...
ROBYN HOOD OF DEADWOOD.	IS DEADWOOD.
ROBYN,	ROBYN,
ROBYN HOOD,	ROBYN HOOD,
ROBYN HOOD OF DEADWOOD,	ROBYN HOOD IS NO GOOD,
ROBYN,	ROBYN,
ROBYN HOOD,	ROBYN HOOD...
ROBYN HOOD OF DEADWOOD,	IS DEADWOOD,
ROBYN HOOD OF DEADWOOD,	ROBYN HOOD IS DEADWOOD,
ROBYN HOOD OF DEADWOOD.	ROBYN HOOD IS DEADWOOD.

(**ROBYN** *enters*)

ROBYN. Hey, Gals. Did you rope us a rich one?

MERRY GALS. Robyn!

MARION. Robyn Hood? But you're a girl!

ROBYN. Do you have a problem with that?

MARION. But I thought…

ROBYN. Yep, a lot of folk think that.

(*to* **LILL**)

So, have you relieved this gentleman of his money?

LILL. Sorry, Robyn. He's just a poor cowpoke name a' Marion Wayne.

(**MERRY GALS** *snigger*)

ROBYN. Sir, I apologise for the poor standard of our hospitality. As we know your name, guess you should know ours. Allow me to introduce our merry band. This is Lillian.

LILL. Lill. Lill John.

ROBYN. This here's Wilhemina Scarlet.

WILL. I prefer to be called Will.

ROBYN. Fryer Tuck.

TUCK. It's Freya, actually. But I'm a demon with a pan, so they call me the fryer.

ROBYN. Over here we have Much Millerson.

MUCH. Really it's Mindy. But they call me that 'cos I don't <u>much</u> about anything.

ROBYN. And this is Eleanor Dale.

MARION. And what do they call you?

ELEANOR. Eleanor Dale.

MARION. Oh.

ROBYN. And then there's Mary, Moira, Mercy, Marcy, Muriel and Euphemia.

MARY/MOIRA/MERCY/MARCY/MURIEL/EUPHEMIA. Howdy, Marion.

ROBYN. Gals, get on back to the camp and get yourselves fed. I'll escort our guest out of the canyon.

BALLADEER BETTY. Boss, are you going to be needing us now?

MARION. Guess not. It'll be strictly solo from now on.

BALLADEER BELLE. Or maybe a duet?

MARION. I ain't the duettin' kind.

(*The* **MERRY GALS** *wish* **MARION** *a safe journey and exit. The* **BALLADEERS** *exit the other way.* **ROBYN** *&* **MARION** *walk into next scene.*)

Scene IV

(ROBYN & MARION walk together.)

ROBYN. So...Marion, right?

MARION. Don't call me that. I hate that name. Call me... Clint.

ROBYN. Clint Wayne. You ain't kin to Duke Wayne by any chance?

MARION. What of it?

ROBYN. Oh, just that our fathers never exactly saw eye to eye.

MARION. So, you're one of them Hoods. No wonder you turned out bad. Just like my pa always said.

ROBYN. I didn't turn out bad.

MARION. Oh, I suppose you think bushwhackin' folk is a fine, upstanding thing to be doin'.

ROBYN. I don't steal off just anyone – only rich cattle barons and such. And I give all the money away to poor people.

MARION. A likely story.

ROBYN. It's true. Why don't you believe me?

MARION. My pa always said you could tell when a Hood was lyin' – 'cos their lips were movin'.

ROBYN. Just 'cos our fathers didn't get along, doesn't mean we can't. We could choose to forgive and forget.

MARION. I ain't the forgivin' or the forgettin' kind.

*(MARION sings. **I DON'T LIKE HOODS/WAYNES**)*

MARION.
> I DON'T LIKE HOODS,
> I DON'T KNOW WHY,
> MY FATHER SAID THAT THEY CHEAT AND LIE,
> AND HERE YOU ARE
> TO PASS THAT TEST,
> THE BIGGEST OUTLAW IN THE WEST,
> UPON HIS KNEE MY PA TAUGHT ME THIS SONG,

THE HOODS AIN'T RIGHT
AND YOU AIN'T PROVED HIM WRONG.

ROBYN. Well, don't you sound like a chip off the old block?
My father warned me about folk like you.

I DON'T LIKE WAYNES,
IT'S IN THE BLOOD,
THE DIRT SURE STICKS WHEN YOU'RE SLINGING MUD,
THEY'RE QUICK TO JUDGE,
AND SLOW TO THINK,
THEY MAKE THEIR MINDS UP IN A BLINK,
I WONDERED IF YOU'D MAYBE BROKE THE MOULD,
BUT YOU'RE A WAYNE,
THAT'S THE WAY THE DICE HAVE ROLLED.

MARION/ROBYN.

WE'LL NEVER AGREE ON ANYTHING…

MARION.

THE LENGTH OF ROPE,

ROBYN.

NO, THE LENGTH OF STRING,

MARION.

IF YOU SAY, 'DAY',

ROBYN.

THEN YOU'LL SAY, 'NIGHT',

MARION.

IF I SAY, 'BLACK',

ROBYN.

THEN I'LL SAY, 'WHITE'.

MARION/ROBYN.

DARN RIGHT!

MARION.

I DON'T LIKE HOODS,

ROBYN.

I DON'T LIKE WAYNES,

MARION.

THEY GOT NO CLASS,

ROBYN.

THEY GOT NO BRAINS,

MARION/ROBYN.

AND THE ONE THING EYE TO EYE WE'LL SEE

IS TO JUST AGREE TO DISAGREE,

THIS COMMON BOND IS SEALED, THE CASE IS SHUT,

ROBYN.

'COS THE WAYNES ARE DOPES,

MARION.

AND THE HOODS ARE A PAIN IN THE...

MARION/ROBYN.

BUT WE'LL FIGHT UNTIL THE SUN DON'T SHINE,

'COS WE JUST DON'T LIKE EACH OTHER,

AND THAT SURE SUITS US FINE.

(**MARION** *&* **ROBYN** *exit different ways*)

Scene V

(Echo Canyon. **SHERIFF**, **GISBOURNE** *&* **DEPUTIES** *enter carrying small sacks of gold.)*

DEPUTY 1. Sheriff, this here's Robyn Hood country.

DEPUTY 2. Folk say there's an outlaw behind every rock.

DEPUTY 3. A bloodthirsty bandit in every tree.

DEPUTY 4. Ready to slit a fella from gullet to gizzard.

DEPUTY 5. John Prince said we should find our own way to Calamity City.

DEPUTY 6. And we should be quick about it.

*(***DEPUTIES*** *exit running.* **SHERIFF** *stops* **GISBOURNE***)*

GISBOURNE. But Sheriff, shouldn't I be heading off this way?

SHERIFF. No, Gisbourne, we'll split up once we're through this canyon.

GISBOURNE. Oh, right. Guess it's safer to travel in pairs through Robyn Hood's territory.

SHERIFF. 'T'ain't that I'm scared. I'd welcome her tryin' to rob me. Give me a chance to capture her and her Merry Gals. I'd be the most feared sheriff in the west. But doesn't hurt to be cautious when carrying a sack of gold.

*(***ROBYN*** *and* **MERRY GALS** *enter and draw catapults)*

ROBYN. Howdy, Sheriff. I couldn't help overhearing something about gold.

GISBOURNE. Sheriff, here's your chance to capture Hood and her gang.

SHERIFF. *(afraid)* Let's not be hasty. There's due process of law. And as yet these young ladies haven't done anything illegal, as far as I can tell.

LILL. That gold seems to be slowing you down quite a bit.

MARY. Why don't we lighten your load a little?

*(***MERRY GALS*** *take their sacks of gold)*

ELEANOR. That is a mighty generous donation to the farmers' benevolent fund.

TUCK. It'll help feed a lot of mouths.

WILL. Let us know when you're passing through again and we'll be sure to give you a warm welcome.

(*mimes cutting her throat*)

MUCH. Yes, stop by for coffee and muffins any time.

ROBYN. And be sure to pass on our regards to John Prince.

(**ROBYN** *&* **MERRY GALS** *exit, laughing*)

GISBOURNE. Shouldn't we chase after them?

SHERIFF. No, it'd be no use. They're well gone by now. Curses! Two more minutes and I'd'a' had her trapped and clapped in irons.

(**ROBYN** *&* **MERRY GALS** *re-enter*)

ROBYN/MERRY GALS. Did you say something, Sheriff?

SHERIFF. Me? Er, no. Not a word. Gisbourne! Run for it!

(**SHERIFF** *and* **GISBOURNE** *exit at speed. During song they enter and exit with* **DEPUTIES**, *getting held up by* **ROBYN** *&* **MERRY GALS** *who sing.* **STICK 'EM UP**)

ROBYN/MERRY GALS.

WHEN A GAL HOLDS AN ACE,
NOT A WORD OUT OF PLACE,
IF SHE GETS IN YOUR FACE,
SIMPLY STICK 'EM UP

'COS SHE WON'T GIVE A HECK,
THAT YOUR DAY'S BEEN A WRECK,
YOU MIGHT JUST SAVE YOUR NECK
IF YOU STICK 'EM UP

ROBYN/MERRY GALS.	**SHERIFF/GISBOURNE/DEPUTIES.**
STICK 'EM UP,	GOTTA RUN,
RAISE YOUR HANDS,	SURE WAS FUN,
STICK 'EM UP.	

ROBYN/MERRY GALS.

IF YOU'VE GOT STACKS OF LOOT,

AND YOU STRAY FROM THE ROUTE,
SHE'LL ASK ONCE THEN SHE'LL SHOOT,
SO GO STICK 'EM UP

SHE DON'T CARE 'BOUT THE LAW,
'COS SHE'S QUICK ON THE DRAW,
LITTLE DOG, RAISE YOUR PAW,
GO ON STICK 'EM UP

ROBYN/MERRY GALS.	**SHERIFF/GISBOURNE/DEPUTIES.**
STICK 'EM UP,	GOTTA RUN,
RAISE YOUR HANDS,	SURE WAS FUN,
GRAB SOME AIR,	BETTER FLY,
BRUSH THE CLOUDS,	THANKS AND 'BYE,
STICK 'EM UP.	

*(**TOWNSFOLK** enter and are given sacks of gold by* **MERRY GALS***)*

ROBYN/MERRY GALS.

WE MUST THANK YOU FOR YOUR GENEROSITY,
ALL THE PEOPLE WILL SHOUT 'HIP-HOORAY!'

TOWNSFOLK.

HIP-HOORAY!

ROBYN/MERRY GALS.

HOW THEY'LL FLOURISH ON YOUR BOUNTI-OCITY,
JUST REMEMBER WHEN YOU'RE NEXT THIS WAY…

ROBYN/MERRY GALS/ **TOWNSFOLK.**	**SHERIFF/GISBOURNE/** **DEPUTIES.**
STICK 'EM UP,	GOTTA RUN,
RAISE YOUR HANDS,	SURE WAS FUN,
GRAB SOME AIR,	BETTER FLY,
BRUSH THE CLOUDS,	THANKS AND 'BYE,
SEIZE THE BLUE,	NEED TO DASH,
PROD THE BIRDS,	KEEP THE CASH,
STICK 'EM UP.	

(During instrumental section, sacks of gold get thrown around, catapults are shot and lots of rowdy stage business happens. All exit. **MARION** *&* **BALLADEERS** *enter.)*

MARION/BALLADEERS.
> I'M/HE'S JUST A WANDERIN' COWBOY
> ENJOYIN' THE QUIET AND PEACE...

> *(**MERRY GALS** & **DEPUTIES** run back on making lots of noise. **MARION** & **BALLADEERS** have to exit in a hurry.)*

ROBYN/MERRY GALS/ TOWNSFOLK.	**SHERIFF/GISBOURNE/ DEPUTIES.**
STICK 'EM UP,	TOUCH THE SKY,
RAISE YOUR HANDS,	LIFT 'EM HIGH,
GRAB SOME AIR,	REACH THE TREES,
BRUSH THE CLOUDS,	CATCH THE BREEZE,
SEIZE THE BLUE,	HOIST YOUR MITTS,
PROD THE BIRDS,	SHOW YOUR PITS,
STICK 'EM UP,	STICK 'EM UP,
STICK 'EM UP,	TOUCH THE SKY,
RAISE YOUR HANDS,	LIFT 'EM HIGH,
GRAB SOME AIR,	REACH THE TREES,
BRUSH THE CLOUDS,	CATCH THE BREEZE,
SEIZE THE BLUE,	HOIST YOUR MITTS,
PROD THE BIRDS,	SHOW YOUR PITS,
STICK 'EM UP,	STICK 'EM UP,
STICK 'EM UP,	STICK 'EM UP,
STICK 'EM UP,	STICK 'EM UP,
STICK 'EM UP.	STICK 'EM UP.

> *(**SHERIFF**, **GISBOURNE** & **DEPUTIES** exit chased by **MERRY GALS** & **TOWNSFOLK**, whooping and hollering)*

Scene VI

(The Indian Village.)

(CHIEF MOUNTAIN LION HEART *sits with rest of* **INDIANS. RUNNING BEAR** *enters in a hurry.)*

RUNNING BEAR. Chief Mountain Lion Heart! Chief Mountain Lion Heart!

CHIEF. Slow down, Running Bear! Why all the hullabaloo?

RUNNING BEAR. Those darn settlers are up to no good again. There are gangs of cowboys rampaging all over the land, raising merry hell.

CHIEF. What is wrong with these people? Can't they just get along? That kind of commotion is very disruptive to the harmony of the land.

RUNNING BEAR. Why don't we chase them off? Run them back east where they belong.

CHIEF. This is a big country, Running Bear. There's room for all kinds of folk in it.

RUNNING BEAR. But they cause us no end of trouble. They scare off the buffalo, they put fences across the prairies, they're always hollering 'yee-haw' and 'yippee-kiy-ay' or some other such nonsense.

CHIEF. Sure, but they've brought us good things as well.

RUNNING BEAR. Such as?

(CHIEF **tries to think.***)*

HOWLING WOLF. Beans?

CHIEF. That's right, Howling Wolf. Everybody loves a bean.

RUNNING BEAR. Okay, beans. But what else?

SQUATTING DOG. Blue jeans?

(INDIANS **nod enthusiastically.***)*

RUNNING BEAR. Alright, beans and blue jeans. But is there anything else?

SQUATTING DOG. I kinda like their coloured beads.

HOWLING WOLF. That's right, Squatting Dog. Those beads sure are pretty.

RUNNING BEAR. *(shaking head in disbelief)* Okay, okay, beans, blue jeans and coloured beads. But what else?

CHIEF. *(hesitating)* I kinda like their music.

RUNNING BEAR. What?! All that whining and wailing?! You actually like that?!

CHIEF. Sure.

RUNNING BEAR. But it's so depressing. Our music's way better.

(**RUNNING BEAR** *and* **INDIANS** *start to chant.*)

CHIEF. Sure, our music's good, but…

(**CHIEF** *sings.* ***THAT IS WHY WE LOVE COUNTRY MUSIC***)

CHIEF/HOWLING WOLF/SQUATTING DOG.
NATIVE AMERICAN INDIANS HAVE SONGS FOR ALL THAT AIL YA,
FROM MINOR INCONVENIENCES TO TOTAL ABJECT FAILURE,
WE'VE SONGS FOR ACHES AND SONGS FOR PAINS
AND ALL THAT'S SENT TO TROUBLE YA,
BUT WE PREFER THE HEARTFELT STRAINS OF GOOD OL' C & W*

SOMETIMES DON'T YOUR LIFE SEEM KINDA CRUMMY?
INDIANS.
KINDA CRUMMY,
CHIEF/HOWLING WOLF/SQUATTING DOG.
MUSIC SOMEHOW HELPS TO SEE IT THROUGH,
INDIANS.
SEE IT THROUGH,
CHIEF/HOWLING WOLF/SQUATTING DOG.
YOU HAVE SUFFERED MANY WRONGS,
BUT WITHIN THOSE COUNTRY SONGS
THERE'LL BE SOME POOR SCHNOOK WHO'S WAY WORSE

---

* Pron. *Double-ya*

OFF THAN YOU

INDIANS.

WORSE OFF THAN YOU

ALL.

AND THAT IS WHY WE LOVE COUNTRY MUSIC,
MAKES US FEEL SO GLAD AND WARM INSIDE,
AT LEAST THE WIFE AIN'T RUN OFF WITH A COWPOKE,
AND AT LEAST YOUR FAV'RITE DOG AIN'T UP AND DIED.

CHIEF/RUNNING BEAR/HOWLING WOLF/SQUATTING DOG.

LIFE CAN SOMETIMES SMACK YOU IN THE KISSER,

INDIANS.

IN THE KISSER,

CHIEF/RUNNING BEAR/HOWLING WOLF/SQUATTING DOG.

FOLK'LL CALL YOU NAMES, THEY'LL SWEAR AND CURSE,

INDIANS.

SWEAR AND CURSE,

CHIEF/RUNNING BEAR/HOWLING WOLF/SQUATTING DOG.

HURTFUL THINGS ARE OFTEN SAID,
'COS YOUR SKIN IS SORTA' RED,
BUT THEM REDNECKS ALWAYS GET IT PLENTY WORSE,

INDIANS.

THEY GET IT WORSE.

ALL.

AND THAT IS WHY WE LOVE COUNTRY MUSIC,
MAKES US FEEL SO GLAD AND WARM INSIDE,
AT LEAST THE WIFE AIN'T RUN OFF,
Y'AINT STAYED UP ALL NIGHT AND CRIED,
AND AT LEAST YOUR FAV'RITE DOG AIN'T UP AND DIED.

AND THAT IS WHY WE LOVE COUNTRY MUSIC,
MAKES US FEEL SO GLAD AND WARM INSIDE,
AT LEAST THE WIFE AIN'T RUN OFF,
AND THE BOSS AIN'T SAID, "YOU'RE FIRED",
YOUR HORSE AIN'T THROWN A SHOE,
YOUR LIFE COVER AIN'T EXPIRED,
YOU HAVEN'T HIT THE BOTTLE,
AIN'T STAYED UP ALL NIGHT AND CRIED,
AND AT LEAST YOUR FAV'RITE DOG…

CHIEF. Spot.

ALL.

> AIN'T UP AND DIED,
> OLD SPOT AIN'T DIED.
>
> *(FX: Dog barks playfully.)*

CHIEF. Attaboy, Spot.

> *(All exit.)*

Scene VII

*(Split scene in Deadwood and **ROBYN**'s hideout. In Deadwood, **JOHN PRINCE** paces while **SHERIFF**, **GISBOURNE** & **DEPUTIES** look on, nervously.)*

JOHN PRINCE. You knuckle-headed numbskulls. How d'ya let yourselves be hoodwinked by a bunch a' girls?

SHERIFF. They're not like normal girls, John. More like wild savages.

GISBOURNE. And they know that canyon like the back of their hands.

JOHN PRINCE. Hmm, so it seems to me we need to draw that Robyn out of her lair so's we can face her…man versus man.

DEPUTY 1. Technically, sir, that'd be man versus <u>girl</u>.

DEPUTY 2. Actually, it'd be <u>men</u> versus girl.

DEPUTY 3. A lot of men.

DEPUTY 4. Versus one girl.

JOHN PRINCE. Whatever! Anyhow, I've the most spectacularly devious idea that's certain to lure her out into the open.

*(They freeze. In **ROBYN**'s hideout, **ROBYN** is thoughtful. **LILL** is reading a poster advertising a 'shooting competition'.)*

LILL. But Robyn, it's the most spectacularly dumb idea I've heard. 'Shooting competition' indeed!

ELEANOR. John Prince can't believe you'll fall for it.

TUCK. It's clearly fixed.

WILL. It's obviously a trap.

MUCH. There are some nice prizes, though.

ROBYN. I'll go in disguise.

MOIRA. But when you win, they're sure to know it's you.

*(**MERRY GALS** agree)*

ROBYN. But I can't have anyone else claiming to be the best shot in Deadwood. I couldn't stand it.

(They freeze. In Deadwood, **JOHN PRINCE** *talks to* **SHERIFF, GISBOURNE** *&* **DEPUTIES***)*

JOHN PRINCE. Robyn Hood won't be able to stand the thought that somebody other than her might be proclaimed the best shot in Deadwood. And when she...

DEPUTY 5. And when she wins, we'll be waiting to nab her!

JOHN PRINCE. That's my line, you noodle-brained nincompoop.

DEPUTY 5. Sorry, Mr. Prince.

*(***TOWNSFOLK** *enter.* **SHARPSHOOTERS** *arrive for the competition carrying catapults.* **GISBOURNE** *takes out paper and pencil)*

SHERIFF. Roll up! Roll up! Test yourselves against the best in the west. See who's the fastest, sharpest sharpshooter in Deadwood.

SHARPSHOOTER X. Where do I sign up for the competition?

GISBOURNE. *(holding out pencil and paper)* Put your name right here, Mister...?

*(***SHARPSHOOTER X** *scratches a large X on the paper)*

Thank you, Mister...*(reads paper)*...Mister X.

*(***GISBOURNE** *is frustrated so hands the paper and pencil to* **DEPUTY 6.** **SHARPSHOOTER DAN** *enters)*

SHARPSHOOTER DAN. I want to enter the shooting competition.

DEPUTY 6. *(about to write name on paper)* What's your name, sir?

SHARPSHOOTER DAN. Call me Dan.

DEPUTY 6. Now I can't just call you Sharpshooter Dan, can I? What's your full name?

SHARPSHOOTER DAN. Dan Arsenlarseningermarsenssen.

DEPUTY 6. *(thinks about writing but gives up)* Okay, you go ahead, Sharpshooter Dan.

(DEPUTY 6 hands paper and pencil to SHERIFF. MARION enters)

MARION. Put my name down for the competition. Tex Wayne.

SHERIFF. Sure thing, Mister Wayne. Now, how do you spell Tex? Oh yeah, M.A.R.I.O.N.

(SHERIFF, GISBOURNE & DEPUTIES snigger. MARION is annoyed)

Is there anybody else who wants to enter the competition to find the finest shot in the whole of the west?

(ROBYN, dressed in Mexican sombrero and poncho and wearing a moustache, enters)

ROBYN. *(attempting Mexican accent)* Si, señor. I take a shot. My name is Pablo Gomez.

SHERIFF. O'Gomez? Irish, eh?

ROBYN. Er, yeah.

JOHN PRINCE. *(eyeing ROBYN suspiciously)* Okay, now we're all set. Let's start the shooting.

SHERIFF. *(secretively to JOHN PRINCE)* But John, Robyn Hood's not here yet.

JOHN PRINCE. *(shaking his head)* Just get on with it.

GISBOURNE. The first round will be the 'can on the fence' shot. Sharpshooters, take your positions.

(SHARPSHOOTER X, SHARPSHOOTER DAN, ROBYN & MARION face the audience and one by one fire their catapults at unseen targets. Each shot hits the target with an FX: Ping)

TOWNSFOLK. *(after each shot)* Hooray!

TOWNSFOLK 1. That is some mighty fine shooting.

TOWNSFOLK 2. I like the look of Dan Arsenlarsenfarsen-harsenmarsen... I like Mister X.

DEPUTY 1. Round two will be the 'moving target'.

(SHARPSHOOTER X hits moving target)

TOWNSFOLK. Hooray!

(**SHARPSHOOTER DAN** *shoots. FX: thud, followed by dog barking in pain*)

TOWNSFOLK. Aw!

TOWNSFOLK 3. Great shot.

TOWNSFOLK 4. What do you mean? He hit the dog.

TOWNSFOLK 3. Yep. I always hated that darn dog.

(**SHARPSHOOTER DAN** *exits with head down.* **ROBYN** *&* **MARION** *complete the round with hits which the* **TOWNSFOLK** *cheer*)

DEPUTY 2. Round three will be the 'can on the window sill'. Careful now, shooters.

(**SHARPSHOOTER X** *shoots. FX: Glass shattering*)

TOWNSFOLK. Aw!

TOWNSFOLK 5. Mrs. Abernathy will sure be pleased.

TOWNSFOLK 6. But that was her window he broke.

TOWNSFOLK 5. But think of the money she'll save on window cleaning.

(**SHARPSHOOTER X** *exits with head down.* **ROBYN** *&* **MARION** *complete the round with hits which the* **TOWNSFOLK** *cheer*)

SHERIFF. People, we have our finalists. Marion… Sorry, <u>Tex</u> Wayne, and Pablo Gomez. For the ultimate test we're going to have the old 'can in the air' shootout. And we'll give extra marks for artistic merit.

TOWNSFOLK. Ooh!

SHERIFF. *(to offstage)* Pull!

(**TOWNSFOLK** *watch the flight of the [unseen] can as* **ROBYN** *shoots three times in successively more complicated fashion – through the legs, round the back of the head, etc. FX: three pings*)

TOWNSFOLK. Hooray!

MARION. Fancy shooting, Señor Gomez.

SHERIFF. *(to offstage)* Pull!

(**TOWNSFOLK** *watch the flight of the [unseen] can as* **MARION** *shoots 3 times in successively more complicated fashion. FX: 2 pings followed by the pained cry of a duck hit in flight*)

TOWNSFOLK. Aw!

MARION. Darn! I just got beat by a Mexican Irishman. I ain't fit to call myself a real cowboy.

JOHN PRINCE. Ladies and gentlemen of Deadwood, I'm pleased to announce we have a winner... Pablo Gomez!

TOWNSFOLK. Hooray!

JOHN PRINCE. And not only that, but I have another important announcement. We have, today, managed to apprehend that notorious bandit – or should that be *bandido*? – Robyn Hood.

(**JOHN PRINCE** *rips off* **ROBYN***'s disguise.* **TOWNSFOLK** *gasp.* **SHERIFF** *&* **DEPUTIES** *surround* **ROBYN** *with their catapults drawn*)

MARION. I got beat by a girl? Robyn, does it give you some kind of kick to humiliate me?

ROBYN. Sorry. I was just so desperate to win the competition.

MARION. Robyn Hood, I hate your guts.

(**MARION** *exits.*)

JOHN PRINCE. *(to* **ROBYN***)* So, Hood, I finally got you.

ROBYN. You may have me, Prince, but when I come before a judge and explain all the wrongs you've done against the people of Deadwood, don't be too sure the law doesn't come down hard on you.

JOHN PRINCE. *(quietly to* **ROBYN***)* That's of course if we get to trial. Say you were to try and... 'escape'. Well, then, the Sheriff here would be perfectly within his rights to shoot you where you stand.

(loudly so everyone can hear)

Sheriff, take this prisoner to the jailhouse. And make sure you lock her up <u>securely</u>.

(**JOHN PRINCE** *exits laughing.*)

SHERIFF. *(grabbing* **ROBYN***'s arm)* Thought you could outsmart me, eh? Thought you'd get the better of Sheriff Nottingham, eh? Well, no one makes me look like an idiot.

GISBOURNE. That's right.

DEPUTIES. You can do that all on your own.

SHERIFF. Exactly… *(realises what they've said)*…Shut up and get this prisoner to jail.

(**SHERIFF** *&* **DEPUTIES** *take* **ROBYN** *across stage.* **MERRY GALS** *enter, dressed as dancing girls.* **SHERIFF** *&* **DEPUTIES** *are stopped in their tracks)*

LILL. Howdy, all! We're the dancin' girls from the Golden Nugget.

DEPUTY 3. Sheriff! Finally, we're gettin' ourselves some dancin' gals!

DEPUTY 4. That means we can get ourselves a Deadwood saloon.

DEPUTY 5. And a Deadwood show!

DEPUTY 6. And a Deadwood stage!

TOWNSFOLK. *(full of wonder)* A Deadwood stage?!

ELEANOR. Sheriff, why don't we give you a little taster of our show?

SHERIFF. Ma'am, I'd be much obliged.

(**MERRY GALS** *sing. **SING & DANCE**)*

MERRY GALS.
WE LADIES ARE HERE TO BRING CULTURE AND MORE,
SOME FINE ENTERTAINMENT, YOU'LL BELLOW, 'ENCORE!'
WE'LL PUT ON A SHOW WITH SOME ELEGANCE AND STYLE
AND WHEN WE HAVE FINISHED, YOU'LL SURE WEAR A SMILE,
OUR DAZZLING TERPSICHORY TURNS HEADS WHEN IT'S SHOWN,
OUR WARBLING IS SURELY THE SWEETEST YOU'VE KNOWN,

WE'LL FLAUNT ALL OUR TALENTS, OUR GIFTS WE'LL
 PARADE
AND MAYBE AN ANKLE MIGHT JUST BE DISPLAYED...

WHEN WE JUST SING AND DANCE FOR NO PARTIC'LAR
REASON,
IT SIMPLY IS THE SEASON TO DO THAT KIND OF THING,
TAKE A CHANCE, YOU'LL FIND IT SORTA' PLEASIN',
TO RAISE A SHOUT AND JIG ABOUT
AND SING AND DANCE AND SING.

SHERIFF. Say, that looks like an awful lot of fun. Gisbourne, what say we get a piece of the action?

*(**SHERIFF**, **GISBOURNE** & **DEPUTIES** join in the dancing with the **MERRY GALS**.)*

SHERIFF/GISBOURNE/DEPUTIES.

IT REALLY IS A TREAT TO GET SOME GLAMOUR IN THIS
PLACE,
WE LOVE TO CUT A RUG, ESPECIALLY WITH A PRETTY FACE,
AND MAYBE WE COULD CUDDLE WHEN THE TEMPO STARTS
TO SLOW,
AND WHERE THE MUSIC TAKES US THEN, YOU NEVER
REALLY KNOW...

CAST.

'COS WE JUST SING AND DANCE FOR NO PARTIC'LAR
REASON,
IT SIMPLY IS THE SEASON TO DO THAT KIND OF THING,
TAKE A CHANCE, YOU'LL FIND IT SORTA' PLEASIN',
TO RAISE A SHOUT AND JIG ABOUT
AND SING AND DANCE AND SING.

*(**MERRY GALS** manoeuvre **SHERIFF**, **GISBOURNE** & **DEPUTIES** so they don't see **WILL** & **TUCK** grab **ROBYN** and exit with her)*

CAST.

SING AND DANCE FOR NO PARTIC'LAR REASON,
IT SIMPLY IS THE SEASON TO DO THAT KIND OF THING,
TAKE A CHANCE, YOU'LL FIND IT SORTA' PLEASIN',
TO RAISE A SHOUT AND JIG ABOUT
AND SING AND DANCE AND SING AND DANCE AND

SING AND DANCE FOR NO PARTIC'LAR REASON,
IT SIMPLY IS THE SEASON TO DO THAT KIND OF THING,
TAKE A CHANCE, YOU'LL FIND IT SORTA' PLEASIN',
TO RAISE A SHOUT AND JIG ABOUT,
MOVE YOUR LIPS AND SHAKE YOUR HIPS,
HOLLER, HOOT AND STAMP YOUR BOOT AND
SING AND DANCE AND
SING AND DANCE AND
SING AND DANCE AND SING…
AND DANCE!

(**MERRY GALS** *exit, followed by* **TOWNSFOLK**.)

Scene VIII

*(Deadwood. **JOHN PRINCE** enters to find **SHERIFF**, **GISBOURNE** & **DEPUTIES** looking around for their prisoner.)*

JOHN PRINCE. *(angry)* Don't tell me. She got away. You had her surrounded. You were yards from the jailhouse. You're armed to the teeth. And somehow she got away! How in tarnt ation could she get away?!

SHERIFF. She tricked us. I told Guy not to trust her but...

GISBOURNE. What?!

SHERIFF. I won't let it happen again, John. Promise. She'll never ever trick me again. When do we go and arrest that varmint?

JOHN PRINCE. We're not going to arrest Robyn Hood, you blithering buffoon.

SHERIFF, GISBOURNE & DEPUTIES. We're not?

JOHN PRINCE. No, we're going to arrest Marion Wayne.

DEPUTY 1. But he hasn't done anything wrong.

JOHN PRINCE. Then make something up. We're going to throw him in jail and wait for Robyn Hood to come and rescue him. Then we'll nab her.

DEPUTY 2. Mister Prince, I don't know if you've noticed, but Hood and Wayne don't get along at all.

DEPUTY 3. That's right, Mister Prince. They hate each other's guts.

JOHN PRINCE. Don't you chuckleheads know anything? When a boy and a girl say they hate each other at the beginning of a story, sure as eggs is eggs, they'll end up getting together by the end. Arresting Marion Wayne will mean the two can do their getting together chaperoned by a bunch of lawmen and a whole heap of bars.

*(**JOHN PRINCE, SHERIFF, GISBOURNE** & **DEPUTIES** hide. **MARION** enters with **BALLADEERS**, singing. WANDERIN' COWBOY – REPRISE)*

MARION.	BALLADEERS.
I'M JUST A WANDERIN' COWBOY,	HE'S JUST A WANDERIN' COWBOY,
LIKE THE BIRDS IN THE TREES,	LIKE THE BIRDS IN THE TREES,
SEE I CAN FLY WHEN I WANT TO,	YES HE CAN FLY WHEN HE WANTS TO...
I'M FREE TO GO WHERE I PLEASE.	

(**SHERIFF, GISBOURNE** *&* **DEPUTIES** *come out from hiding place.* **JOHN PRINCE** *watches from the side*)

SHERIFF. Stop right there, Wayne.

MARION. *(to audience)* I sometimes wonder if I'm ever going to finish this darn song.

(to **SHERIFF***)*

What is it now?

SHERIFF. You're under arrest.

MARION. Under arrest? What the heck for?

SHERIFF. *(thinks)* Tell him, Guy.

GISBOURNE. What? Oh, for singing on a Sunday.

SHERIFF. That's right. God's day should not be defiled by non-church-type songs. We're arresting you for singing on a Sunday.

BALLADEER BETTY. Sheriff, today is Saturday.

GISBOURNE. Oops.

(**SHERIFF** *can't think, so motions to* **DEPUTY 4**)

DEPUTY 4. Then you're under arrest for... jaywalking.

BALLADEER BELLE. Now how can he be jaywalking when Deadwood doesn't even have any sidewalks?

SHERIFF. Now hush up, you Balladeers. It's strictly a singing role, remember.

(to **MARION***)*

Marion Wayne, you're under arrest for walking the wrong way down a one-way street.

MARION. You dopes better come up with something a lot smarter if you're thinking of locking me away.

(**JOHN PRINCE** *comes up behind* **MARION** *and strikes him on the back of the head.* **MARION** *falls, unconscious*)

JOHN PRINCE. Sheriff, I do believe this gentleman is asleep on a public highway.

DEPUTY 5. That's a clear charge of vagrancy.

DEPUTY 6. You're coming with us, you dirty lawbreaker.

(**DEPUTIES** *help* **MARION** *up and take him to the jailhouse. They exit.*)

BALLADEER BETTY. So what do we do now?

BALLADEER BELLE. Find us a new singing cowboy, I guess.

(**BALLADEERS** *exit.*)

Scene IX

(Int/Ext jailhouse – night. **MARION** *sits in jail (in spotlight or behind wall).* **ROBYN** *enters and they talk as if she's on the other side of the wall and they can't see each other.)*

ROBYN. Marion? I mean, Butch. No, Clint. Tex? You in there?

MARION. 'Course I'm in here. And I deserve to be in here after letting those numb-nuts, Nottingham and Gisbourne, arrest me. I ain't fit to call myself a real cowboy.

ROBYN. Don't be too hard on yourself. John Prince is behind all this, and he's one sneaky operator.

MARION. Then you should be careful. What are you doin' in town?

ROBYN. I came to break you outta jail.

MARION. Me? But why would you risk yourself for me? – A Wayne.

ROBYN. I dunno. Guess… Oh, I dunno.

    *(***ROBYN*** sings.* ***I DON'T MIND WAYNES/HOODS****)*

ROBYN.
    I DON'T MIND WAYNES,
    THEY AIN'T SO BAD,
    YOU GET TO KNOW 'EM AND YOU'RE LIKELY GLAD,
MARION.
    AND HOODS JUST SEEM TO GET BAD PRESS,
    BUT THAT DON'T RATE 'EM ANY LESS,
ROBYN.
    THE COVER DON'T TELL BUT HALF OF THE PLOT,
MARION.
    AND HALF A BOOK IS SOME, BUT NOT A LOT.

MARION.

I'M JUST A WANDERIN'
COWBOY,
WITH THOUGHTS OF
SETTLIN' DOWN,
IF I COULD FIND ME A
REASON,
AND I COULD FIND ME A
TOWN,
WOULDN'T NEED TO WEAR
A FROWN,

ROBYN.

THIS STUFF 'BOUT WAYNES
IS JUST PLAIN OLD,
I KNOW OF ONE WHO
BREAKS THE MOULD,
AND IF THERE'S ONE,
THERE'S LIKELY MORE,
AND IF THERE'S MORE I
KNOW FOR SURE

ROBYN/MARION.

THIS MIGHT JUST BE THE START OF SOMETHING NEW,

MARION.

IF THE HOODS AND WAYNES COULD BE LIKE ME AND YOU,

ROBYN.

LIKE YOU AND I,

ROBYN/MARION.

WE'D SURE GET BY.

(**ROBYN** *hears something and hides*)

(**MERRY GALS** *enter dressed as respectable ladies of the town.* **TUCK** *carries a cake*)

LILL. Sheriff! Oh, Sheriff! Are you in there, Sheriff?

(**SHERIFF**, **GISBOURNE** *&* **DEPUTIES** *enter*)

SHERIFF. Who's out there? What do you want?

LILL. Why, Sheriff, we are the Deadwood Ladies Prison Welfare League.

ELEANOR. We are seriously concerned about the prisoners in our system.

TUCK. So we've baked a cake to keep their spirits up with some good home cooking.

(**SHERIFF** *nudges* **GISBOURNE** *– aware of some kind of ruse*)

SHERIFF. A cake, eh?

GISBOURNE. *(laughs knowingly)* Cake.

(to SHERIFF, *confused)*

What's wrong with a cake?

SHERIFF. *(quietly to* GISBOURNE*)* Don't you know the old file-hidden-in-the-cake routine? It's the oldest trick in the book. They sneak in a file, baked inside a cake, so the prisoner can cut through the bars. But we ain't falling for that scam. No, siree.

(to MERRY GALS*)*

Reckon we might have to try that cake to check the ingredients.

TUCK. Be my guest, Sheriff.

(SHERIFF, GISBOURNE *&* DEPUTIES *devour cake)*

ELEANOR. Well, how do you like it?

SHERIFF. *(frustrated he can't find a file)* Come on. Out with it. What have you got in this here cake?

TUCK. Why, nothing out of the ordinary. Some sugar, eggs, flour, molasses... oh, and some Indian sleeping powder.

GISBOURNE. Indian sleeping powder?

SHERIFF. What in tarnation is Indian sleeping powww...?

(at that moment, SHERIFF, GISBOURNE *&* DEPUTIES *all fall immediately asleep)*

ROBYN. *(coming out from hiding)* Let's free the prisoner, gals.

(MERRY GALS *help* MARION *from the jailhouse)*

WILL. I still say we should have forced our way in, blown the bars and shot our way out.

MARION. I ain't the thankin' kind, but I just want to say I appreciate what you gals done for me.

TUCK. 'T'weren't nothin'. I do love to bake.

MARY. What do you think John Prince will do now, Robyn?

MOIRA. He'll be mighty mad.

MERCY. And looking to get even.

ROBYN. Whatever he tries, we'll be ready for it. Marcy, where'd you tether the horses?

MARCY. Just over the way there.

(**MARCY** *points offstage. FX: horses neigh*)

ROBYN. Well let's get outta here before these fellas start waking up.

MUCH. I just want to grab me some of that cake.

(**ROBYN** *pulls* **MUCH** *away from the cake before she can eat any.* **ROBYN, MARION** *&* **MERRY GALS** *exit*)

MUCH. *(cont. over exit)* But it looks so delicious.

Scene X

(Split scene: Deadwood & **ROBYN***'s hideout. In Deadwood,* **JOHN PRINCE** *paces while* **SHERIFF**, **GISBOURNE** *&* **DEPUTIES** *wait.)*

JOHN PRINCE. That does it. There's only one thing to do now.

SHERIFF. That's right. Go in, all guns blazin'…

DEPUTY 1. Burn the land…

DEPUTY 2. Dynamite the rocks…

DEPUTY 3. Ride roughshod over the whole darn territory.

JOHN PRINCE. No, you blundering bumblebrains! I'm gonna have to go legit.

SHERIFF. Aw, John, legit's no fun. We'll have to do things by the book.

DEPUTY 4. No bribes…

DEPUTY 5. No brutality…

DEPUTY 6. No backhanders…

GISBOURNE. And just think of all that paperwork.

JOHN PRINCE. My mind's made up. I'm gonna run for mayor. Once this town has a mayor, we'll be on the map. And that means we can call in government help. Heck, we could even call for the 7th Cavalry. Not even Robyn Hood can stand up to the 7th Cavalry.

(In **ROBYN***'s hideout,* **ROBYN** *paces while* **MERRY GALS** *&* **MARION** *look concerned)*

ROBYN. John Prince? Mayor of Deadwood? Somebody has to stop him.

MARION. Nobody'll vote for that crook.

ROBYN. He'll <u>buy</u> enough votes – unless somebody stands against him.

LILL. But who's gonna be dumb enough to do that?

TUCK. Likely, John Prince would use every rotten trick in the book.

WILL. He'd use dirty smears…

MURIEL. He'd use character assassination…

EUPHEMIA. He'd use regular assassination.

ROBYN. I'm going to have to stand against him.

MARION. That surely gets some kinda prize – as the lamest idea ever.

ROBYN. Why? Don't you think I could win?

MARION. Of course. But to accept the post, you'd have to declare yourself in town. And then Prince would have you exactly where he wanted.

ELEANOR. He's right, Robyn. It's too dangerous.

ROBYN. If I don't stand, he'll have a clear run. It's time I stopped hiding in the shadows. It's time I went face to face with John Prince and found out who's the better man.

(**MARION** & **MERRY GALS** *are confused*)

ROBYN. *(cont.)* Well, you know what I mean.

(*They exit. In Deadwood,* **TOWNSFOLK** *enter as* **JOHN PRINCE** *and* **DEPUTIES** *sing* ***VOTE FOR ME***)

JOHN PRINCE.
VOTE FOR ME, VOTE FOR ME, VOTE FOR ME,
DEPUTIES.
AND A CUT IN ALL YOUR TAXES HE'LL PROVIDE,
JOHN PRINCE.
VOTE FOR ME, VOTE FOR ME, VOTE FOR ME,
DEPUTIES.
LOTS OF MONEY FOR YOURSELVES AND MORE BESIDE,
JOHN PRINCE.
VOTE FOR ME, VOTE FOR ME, VOTE FOR ME,
DEPUTIES.
LET YOUR POCKET NOT YOUR CONSCIENCE BE YOUR
    GUIDE;
BE YOU LEFT OR RIGHT OR CENTRE,
A POLITICAL DISSENTER,
YOUR ELECTED REPRESENTER HE WILL BE,
BE SMART…

JOHN PRINCE.

> VOTE FOR ME.

> (**JOHN PRINCE** *goes about shaking hands.* **SHERIFF** *&* **DEPUTIES** *menace the* **TOWNSFOLK**)

SHERIFF/GISBOURNE/DEPUTIES.   **JOHN PRINCE.**

VOTE FOR HIM, VOTE FOR HIM, VOTE FOR HIM,	VOTE FOR ME!
AND THE PROBLEMS THAT YOU FACE WILL DISAPPEAR,	THEY'LL DISAPPEAR!
VOTE FOR HIM, VOTE FOR HIM, VOTE FOR HIM,	THAT'S ME!
AND YOUR LIVES WILL BE MUCH BETTER, DON'T'CHA HEAR?	AIN'T YA LISTENING?!
VOTE FOR HIM, VOTE FOR HIM, VOTE FOR HIM,	JOHN PRINCE!
IF WE CAN'T INSPIRE TRUST WE'LL STRIKE SOME FEAR,	THE MAN TO FEAR...
WE'LL BE NICE AND THEN WE'LL THREATEN,	ER... TRUST!
PRETTY SOON WE'LL HAVE YOU SWEATIN',	
YOUR SURVIVAL CHANCES GETTING' KINDA SLIM,	
BE SMART...	YOU KNOW IT MAKES
VOTE FOR HIM.	SENSE!

(ALT. LYRIC: VOTE FOR HER, VOTE FOR HER, VOTE FOR HER, AND THE PROBLEMS THAT YOU FACE WILL DISAPPEAR, VOTE FOR HER, VOTE FOR HER, VOTE FOR HER, AND YOUR LIVES WILL BE MUCH BETTER, DON'T'CHA HEAR? VOTE FOR HER, VOTE FOR HER, VOTE FOR HER, IF WE CAN'T INSPIRE TRUST WE'LL STRIKE SOME FEAR, WE'LL BE NICE AND THEN WE'LL THREATEN, PRETTY SOON WE'LL HAVE YOU SWEATIN', LIKE IT'S SUMMERTIME AND YOU ARE DRESSED IN FUR, BE SMART... VOTE FOR HER.)

(**ROBYN** *&* **MERRY GALS** *enter*)

ROBYN.

VOTE FOR ME,

MERRY GALS.

AND END THIS CRUEL OPPRESSION,

ROBYN.

VOTE FOR ME,

MERRY GALS.

AND RAISE US FROM DEPRESSION,

ROBYN.

VOTE FOR ME,

ROBYN/MERRY GALS.

EACH CROSS MAKES AN IMPRESSION,
MIGHT CAN NEVER FIGHT
THE ONE WHO'S RIGHT
AND BEARS THE LIGHT
OF TRUTH AND OF JUSTICE
AND GOOD OL' HONESTY,

ROBYN.

VOTE FOR ME.

*(On two sides of the stage, **ROBYN** and **JOHN PRINCE** lead their followers in a march to victory.)*

MERRY GALS/TOWNSFOLK 1.	**SHERIFF, ETC./TOWNSFOLK 2.**
VOTE FOR HOOD,	VOTE FOR PRINCE, VOTE FOR PRINCE, VOTE FOR PRINCE,
THOSE BOOKS SHE WON'T BE COOKING,	AND THE PROBLEMS THAT YOU FACE WILL DISAPPEAR,
VOTE FOR HOOD,	VOTE FOR PRINCE, VOTE FOR PRINCE, VOTE FOR PRINCE,

NO ARGUMENTS WE'RE
BROOKING,

VOTE FOR HOOD,

SHE'S ALSO BETTER
LOOKING,
SHOUT YOUR MESSAGE
OUT,
WITHOUT A DOUBT WE'LL
CAUSE A ROUT,

LET'S SEND UP A SIGN
THAT WILL

BE UNDERSTOOD,
VOTE FOR HOOD,

VOTE FOR HOOD,

VOTE FOR HOOD,
HOOD,
HOOD,
HOOD,
PRINCE,
PRINCE,
HOOD!
GOOD!

AND YOUR LIVES WILL
BE MUCH BETTER,
DON'T'CHA HEAR?
VOTE FOR PRINCE, VOTE
FOR PRINCE, VOTE FOR
PRINCE,
IF WE CAN'T INSPIRE TRUST
WE'LL STRIKE SOME FEAR,
WE'LL BE NICE AND THEN
WE'LL THREATEN,
PRETTY SOON WE'LL HAVE
YOU SWEATIN',
LIKE YOUR CLOTHES ARE
GONNA NEED AN EXTRA
RINSE,

BE SMART…

VOTE FOR PRINCE,

VOTE FOR PRINCE,
PRINCE,
PRINCE,
PRINCE,
PRINCE,
HOOD,
HOOD,
HOOD!
GOOD!

(**ROBYN, MERRY GALS** *&* **GISBOURNE** *exit*)

Scene XI

(Deadwood. **JOHN PRINCE, SHERIFF, DEPUTIES** *&*
TOWNSFOLK *await the result of the vote. Nobody has a
catapult.* **MARION** *enters, disguised as a little old lady,
shielding his face behind a veil, carrying a handbag.)*

TOWNSFOLK 1. So, who did you vote for?

TOWNSFOLK 2. I voted for John Prince.

TOWNSFOLK 3. For his tough stand on law and order?

TOWNSFOLK 2. Mm-hm.

TOWNSFOLK 4. I voted for Robyn Hood.

TOWNSFOLK 5. For her tough stand on John Prince?

TOWNSFOLK 4. Mm-hm.

TOWNSFOLK 6. I can't be sure, but I think I voted for
Mister X.

SHERIFF. Ladies and gentlemen of Deadwood, we are
about to announce the winner of the election to find
the new mayor of Deadwood. This historic occasion
deserves a few words to explain the importance of the
democratic system to our young nation…

JOHN PRINCE. Get on with it, pin-head.

SHERIFF. Sorry, John. Deputy Guy Gisbourne, come forward
with the voting results, which have been carefully
collated… With no hint of finaglin' or funny business.

*(GISBOURNE enters carrying an envelope. He tears it
open and takes out a sheet of paper.)*

GISBOURNE. The new mayor of Deadwood is Joh…

(reads paper)

Robyn Hood!

(TOWNSFOLK cheer.)

SHERIFF. Robyn Hood?!

JOHN PRINCE. Robyn Hood?! This can't be! What on earth's
this country coming to when you can't fix an election?

Anyhow, no matter. You have to be here to accept the position, and as I'm the only candidate here…

(**ROBYN** *&* **MERRY GALS** *enter – without catapults.*)

ROBYN & MERRY GALS. Not so fast, Prince.

(**TOWNSFOLK** *cheer.*)

ROBYN. As the rightful winner of the election, I'm here to claim my position as mayor of Deadwood.

JOHN PRINCE. But as you haven't been sworn in yet, you're just a common citizen and, as such, can be shot for the criminal you are. Sheriff, shoot that hornswoggling thief!

ROBYN. You're forgetting, Prince. This is an election, and so nobody is allowed weapons.

JOHN PRINCE. Nobody?

ROBYN. Nobody.

JOHN PRINCE. So, I guess I should have handed this in somewhere.

(**JOHN PRINCE** *pulls out catapult from inside his jacket.* **TOWNSFOLK** *gasp.*)

LILL. Watch out, Robyn!

TUCK. You dirty rat, Prince!

ELEANOR. He's packing heat!

WILL. And he's just about crazy enough to use it!

MUCH. Now that's just not fair!

MARY/MOIRA/MERCY/MARCY/MURIEL/EUPHEMIA. Run for it, Robyn!

ROBYN. If I run then I'm no better than the coward holding the weapon.

JOHN PRINCE. *(aiming catapult)* I've waited a long time for this, Robyn Hood.

MARION. *(to* **PRINCE** *– as old lady)* Excuse me, sonny.

JOHN PRINCE. Get lost. Grandma.

(**JOHN PRINCE** *goes to fire*)

MARION. Now that ain't a nice way to talk to a lady.

(MARION strikes JOHN PRINCE with his handbag. JOHN PRINCE falls to the floor)

MARION. *(cont. taking horseshoe from handbag and pulling off veil)* Dang! I finally got the chance to prove myself as a real, honest-to-goodness, red-blooded cowboy.

TOWNSFOLK. Well, sorta'.

ROBYN. Thanks, Marion.

MARION. Robyn, I told you – I ain't the Marion kind.

ROBYN. Well who said anything about getting married?!

TOWNSFOLK/MERRY GALS. Aw!

(ROBYN and MARION realise their mistake and shrug.)

JOHN PRINCE. What is all this horse-poop?! Sheriff, Gisbourne, Deputies! Get those gals!

(All run to grab a sack/pillow from the pile stacked upstage. A big pillow fight ensues. This continues until a bugle is heard offstage)

JOHN PRINCE. You're finished, Robyn Hood. Here comes the 7th Cavalry.

(INDIANS enter and all drop their sacks/pillows, a little embarrassed. RUNNING BEAR carries a trumpet)

CHIEF. Leave the horses here, guys.

(FX: Horses neigh)

SHERIFF. Injuns? But that's a cavalry bugle?

RUNNING BEAR. I guess you haven't heard of the Little Big Horn.

JOHN PRINCE. But how?

CHIEF. *(raising hand in greeting)* Well, 'How' yourself.

ROBYN. Chief Mountain Lion Heart, what brings you to our peaceful little town?

CHIEF. Peaceful?

HOWLING WOLF. You settlers don't know the meaning of the word.

SQUATTING DOG. We can hear that commotion all the way over the other side of Loxley County.

RUNNING BEAR. If you can't keep a lid on things, we're going to have to kick you back east where you belong.

CHIEF. We're telling you, Robyn Hood, because it's your responsibility as mayor.

JOHN PRINCE. But the election was rigged! She's a criminal! I demand a recount!

RUNNING BEAR. Don't give us any of your lip, Prince. We still like to do the odd spot of hair trimming – if you get my drift.

(**JOHN PRINCE** *shuts up.*)

ROBYN. Sorry, Chief. It'll be my first act as mayor of Deadwood to ensure we have a lawman strong enough to really keep the peace.

(*turns to* **MARION**)

Sir, how would you like to change your name to <u>Sheriff</u> Wayne?

MARION. Sheriff Wayne? I think I'd like that.

(*He takes badge from* **SHERIFF** *and pins it on himself.*)

SHERIFF. Aw, darn. And I liked bein' sheriff.

GISBOURNE. Can I get to stay on as deputy?

MARION. Well, let me think. You locked me up under false charges, you tried to kill Robyn Hood and you helped rig an election. I guess it'd be okay if you stayed on in the jailhouse – behind bars.

GISBOURNE. But I was only following orders from John Prince and Sheriff Nottingham.

MARION. Anybody else fancy testifying against Prince and the sheriff?

DEPUTIES. Sure thing!

MARION. And that's about all the witnesses I need to make my first arrests. John Prince, Sheriff Nottingham, I'm taking you in.

ROBYN. And with John Prince behind bars, he won't be needing my parents' farm any more.

MARION. Guess not.

ROBYN HOOD. And when we pan the gold from that river, there'll be money to buy this town what it really needs.

LILL/ELEANOR. Like a schoolhouse…

TUCK/WILL. And a library…

MARY/MOIRA/MARCY. A decent canteen…

MERCY/MURIEL/EUPHEMIA. And a railroad link…

MUCH. And stables so we can finally tether the horses in town.

TOWNSFOLK. Darn right!

(FX: Horses neigh)

ROBYN. *(to CHIEF)* So, what do you propose we do now?

CHIEF. Well, if it was up to me, I'd end this thing with a song.

TOWNSFOLK. Why?

CHIEF. Ah, no particular reason.

*(All sing. **SING & DANCE** – Reprise)*

CAST.

> SING AND DANCE FOR NO PARTIC'LAR REASON,
> IT SIMPLY IS THE SEASON TO DO THAT KIND OF THING,
> TAKE A CHANCE, YOU'LL FIND IT SORTA' PLEASIN',
> TO RAISE A SHOUT AND JIG ABOUT
> AND SING AND DANCE AND SING. (CHORUS X2)

> IT'S GOOD TO KNOW THE SETTLERS ARE FIN'LY SETTLIN' DOWN,
> AND GREAT TO REALLY GET SOME LAW AND ORDER IN THIS TOWN,

IT'S TIME TO PUT AWAY OUR GUNS 'COS EVERYTHING IS
RIGHT,
AND BEST OF ALL WE GET TO THROW A PARTY WHERE WE
MIGHT JUST HAVE TO...

SING AND DANCE FOR NO PARTIC'LAR REASON,
IT SIMPLY IS THE SEASON TO DO THAT KIND OF THING,
TAKE A CHANCE, YOU'LL FIND IT SORTA' PLEASIN',
TO RAISE A SHOUT AND JIG ABOUT
AND SING AND DANCE AND SING.

SING FOR THE NEW LAWMAN,
SING FOR THE INDIAN BRAVE,
SING FOR THE GALS WHO WON THE WEST
AND SING FOR THE ONE WHO SENT INJUSTICE TO ITS
GRAVE...

(CHORUS 1)   *(CHORUS 2)*

(CHORUS 1)	(CHORUS 2)
AND THE NAME IS ROBYN,	ROBYN,
ROBYN HOOD,	ROBYN HOOD,
ROBYN HOOD OF DEADWOOD,	ROBYN HOOD OF DEADWOOD,
ROBYN,	ROBYN,
ROBYN HOOD,	ROBYN HOOD,
ROBYN HOOD OF DEADWOOD,	OF DEADWOOD,
ROBYN,	ROBYN,
ROBYN HOOD,	ROBYN HOOD,
ROBYN HOOD OF DEADWOOD,	ROBYN HOOD OF DEADWOOD,
ROBYN,	ROBYN,
ROBYN HOOD,	ROBYN HOOD,
ROBYN HOOD OF DEADWOOD,	OF DEADWOOD,
ROBYN HOOD OF DEADWOOD,	ROBYN HOOD OF DEADWOOD,
ROBYN HOOD OF DEADWOOD.	ROBYN HOOD OF DEADWOOD.

The End